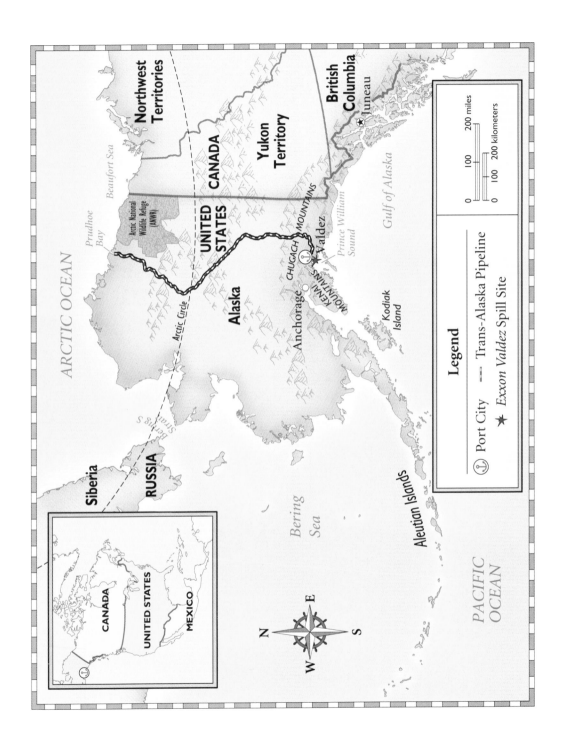

# DESTINATION VALDEZ

by Nancy Warren Ferrell

Lerner Publications Company • Minneapolis

## PHOTO ACKNOWLEDGMENTS

Cover photograph by Harry M. Walker. All inside photos © Harry M. Walker, pp. 5, 18, 19, 20, 24 (left), 27, 41, 42, 56, 66, 67, 72, 73; © Sigal Ashley, Valdez, AK, pp. 6, 64, 70, 76; © Ron Levy, pp. 8, 17, 30, 59, 74; © William B. Folsom, pp. 9, 14, 24 (right), 35, 54; © Paul A. Souders, pp. 10–11, 22–23, 25, 26, 28, 46, 50, 63, 69; by Paul Giraudin, courtesy of Valdez Convention and Visitors Bureau, p. 15; courtesy of Prints Division, New York Public Library, Astor, Lenox and Tilden Foundations, p. 31; courtesy of State of Alaska Department of Education, p. 32 (both); courtesy of Bancroft Library, University of California, p. 34; courtesy of National Archives of Canada, neg. no. PA126210, p. 36; courtesy of Alaska State Library, U.S. Army Signal Corps Collection photo no. PCA 175-13, p. 38; courtesy of Alaska State Library, National Archives 94-x-16, photo no. PCA 175-36, p. 39; courtesy of Alyeska Pipeline Service Company, pp. 44, 58; UPI/Corbis-Bettmann, p. 45; courtesy of National Geophysical Data Center, p. 43; courtesy of Oil Spill Public Information Center, p. 47; © Michele Burgess, p. 49; Archive Photos/Thompson, p. 55; © Bob Benda, p. 60; © Erwin C. 'Bud' Nielsen/Images International, p. 61; © William McCloskey, p. 71; © Ace Kvale, p. 75. Maps by Ortelius Design.

*This book is dedicated to my Juneau, Alaska, writing group: Jean Rogers, Susi Gregg Fowler, Bridget Smith, and, through correspondence, Dale DeArmond. All are longtime Alaskans, professionals, and friends.*

Website address: www.lernerbooks.com

LIBRARY OF CONGRESS CATALOGING-IN-PUBLICATION DATA

Ferrell, Nancy Warren.
    Destination Valdez / by Nancy Warren Ferrell.
       p. cm. — (Port cities of North America)
    Includes index.
    Summary: Discusses the geography, history, economy, and daily life of the Alaskan port city of Valdez.
     ISBN 0-8225-2790-1 (lib. bdg. : alk. paper)
     1. Valdez (Alaska)—Juvenile literature. [1. Valdez (Alaska)] I. Title. II. Series.
F914.V3F47 1998
979.8'3—dc21                    97–4211

Manufactured in the United States of America
1 2 3 4 5 6 – JR – 03 02 01 00 99 98

The quote on page 69 comes from *Alaska Geographic* Volume 20, Number 1, *Prince William Sound,* page 43. © 1993 Alaska Geographic Society.

The glossary that begins on page 76 gives definitions of words shown in **bold type** in the text.

# CONTENTS

# CHAPTER ONE

# NEAR THE TOP OF THE WORLD

*The lights of the Alyeska Marine Terminal, Valdez's oil facility, glitter on the mountainside as a supertanker receives a cargo of crude oil.*

The Port of Valdez, Alaska, nestles in a narrow inlet of Prince William Sound among mountains and **glaciers.** To the south, the sound opens into the Gulf of Alaska, part of the Pacific Ocean. The Arctic Circle, an imaginary line marking the boundary of the northern polar region, lies about 400 miles to the north. Farther north Alaska's North Slope (northern coastal plain) meets the Beaufort Sea—an arm of the Arctic Ocean. Canada's Yukon Territory is 180 miles east of the port. About 1,000 miles west of Valdez, across the Bering Strait, lies a part of Russia called Siberia. Long stretches of wilderness separate Valdez from neighboring towns— a distance of 109 miles to Glenallen by road and 85 miles to Cordova by sea.

*Shoup Glacier flows between two peaks in the Chugach Mountains northwest of Valdez. The thick, heavy ice moves like a liquid, but much more slowly.*

Prince William Sound is a huge saltwater basin rimmed by two mountain ranges—the Kenai Mountains on the west and the Chugach Mountains on the north and east—and surrounded by ice fields and glaciers. These formations are remnants of the Pleistocene Epoch, or Ice Age, which ended 10,000 years ago.

During the Ice Age, ice towered high around the area of the sound. The glaciers gouged out valleys and **fjords** as they scraped across the land. Glacial activity created the sound and its many canals, straits, bays, inlets, and islands. The ice also carved a harbor deep enough for docking the massive oil supertankers that make Valdez a major port. Smaller remnants of the Ice Age glaciers, such as Valdez Glacier to the north of the port and Columbia Glacier to the west, still lie among the mountains.

The Chugach Mountains rise 7,000 feet above sea level and protect the town and port from extreme weather moving down from the

➤ If the shorelines of Prince William Sound's many fjords, islands, bays, and inlets were stretched out into a straight line, the line would reach from Valdez to Los Angeles, California—a distance of more than 3,500 miles.

north. Because of this mountainous barrier, Valdez tends to be neither as warm nor as cold as other parts of Alaska. In January, the coldest month, the temperature averages 25° F. July is normally the warmest month, with temperatures around 55° F. When the sun shines and the sky is clear, the scenery around Valdez is spectacular, with endless snowy peaks and green alpine forests. Although Valdez is sheltered from direct coastal exposure, ocean winds frequently blow through the sound—often bringing rain or snow. Low clouds and fog sometimes hang over the port.

**A World-Class Port** ➤ Valdez is the number one crude oil port in the United States. In fact, Valdez boasts the largest oil terminal in North America. And Valdez is

*On a foggy, gray day, piles of logs sit at the General Cargo and Container Wharf, the main non-oil export facility at Valdez.*

the fifth largest U.S. port in terms of overall tonnage handled each year. Only the ports of Baton Rouge, South Louisiana, Houston, and New York deal with more.

Ships approaching Valdez might enter Prince William Sound through Montague Strait in the southwest or through Hinchinbrook Entrance in the southeast. Boats sail across the sound past numerous islands—such as Goose, Bligh, and Glacier—to Valdez Arm, a 12-mile-long saltwater fjord. Vessels then navigate Valdez Narrows—a passage connecting the arm to the port. An eastward turn brings vessels into the port, which is 12 miles long east to west and 3 miles north to south. Located on the northern shore of the port is the town of Valdez.

The Port of Valdez is unusual because of the depth of its harbor—900 feet deep in the middle. Shaped like a huge whale, the port narrows and becomes shallower at the "whale's tail,"or the western end that meets Valdez Narrows. The narrows is a half mile wide and 350 feet deep, allowing ship traffic to move only one way at a time. A system of light towers, radar beacons, fog signals, buoys, and day markers helps guide the way in and out of the port.

Valdez Narrows is shallower than other areas of the port, but the passage can still easily ac-

*A supertanker makes its way through Valdez Narrows.*

commodate huge supertankers. The water is also deep enough to prevent the port from freezing during the cold winters, making the Port of Valdez the northernmost ice-free harbor in North America.

Although Valdez is accessible by many forms of transportation, travelers don't just accidentally happen upon the city on their way somewhere else. Valdez takes some effort to reach. Every day airplanes come from Alaska's largest cities, Anchorage and Fairbanks, landing on the 6,500-foot paved airstrip outside of town. A flight from Anchorage to Valdez takes only about 40 minutes. Drivers can take the scenic, all-weather Richardson Highway. The Richardson starts in Valdez and connects with roads leading north to Fairbanks, west to Anchorage, and east to the Alaska Highway, which runs through Canada.

**The Two Harbors** ➤ The Port of Valdez has two harbors—Valdez Harbor, also called the downtown harbor, and the Alyeska Marine Terminal, or Alyeska harbor. The downtown harbor is a way station for tourists in the summer. Throughout the year, this harbor also handles cargo such as seafood, logs, and construction materials. Seven city employees direct harbor and port activities. A director governs the harbor with help from port and harbor commissioners, the city manager, and the city council. Together they make decisions pertaining to the commercial docks, marina, and airport. In 1995 these facilities earned more than $1 million in revenues.

The community does a great deal to serve travelers of all kinds. Valdez has marine repair

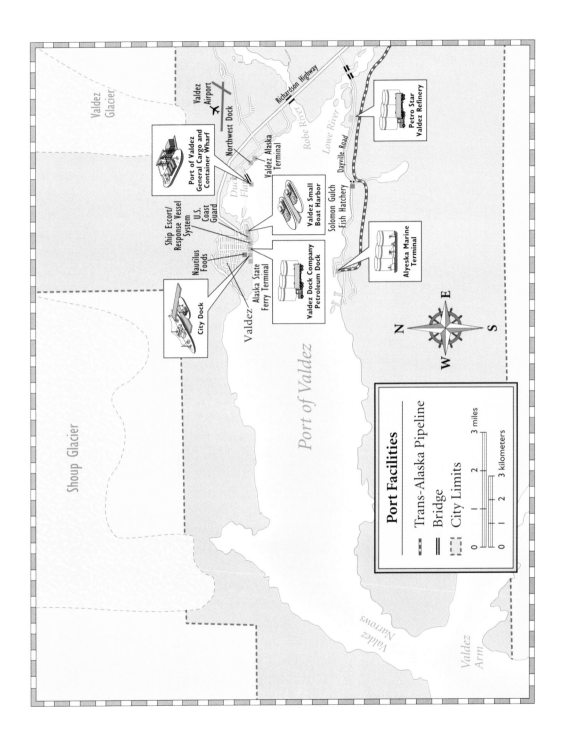

Port of Valdez

Shoup Glacier

Valdez Glacier

Valdez Airport

Northwest Dock

Richardson Highway

Robe River

Lowe River

Valdez Alaska Terminal

Port of Valdez General Cargo and Container Wharf

Ship Escort/Response Vessel System

U.S. Coast Guard

Valdez Small Boat Harbor

Solomon Gulch Fish Hatchery

Dayville Road

Petro Star Valdez Refinery

Nautilus Foods

Valdez

Alaska State Ferry Terminal

Valdez Dock Company Petroleum Dock

Alyeska Marine Terminal

City Dock

Valdez Narrows

Valdez Arm

N E S W

**Port Facilities**

Trans-Alaska Pipeline

Bridge

City Limits

0    1    2    3 miles

0    1    2    3 kilometers

shops, fueling stations, and restaurants along its shore. The downtown harbor also hosts frequent stops of the Alaska State Ferry. The ferries sail to other towns on Prince William Sound, as well as to Seward and Kodiak on the Gulf of Alaska and to Homer on Cook Inlet. Ferries stop in Valdez almost every day in the summer and twice weekly in the winter. In 1996 more than 13,700 people stepped off the ferry and onto the Alaska State Ferry Terminal, a dock made of galvanized metal, or onto the older, wooden City Dock. The City Dock also receives hauls of seafood from commercial fishing boats. The catches go to Nautilus Foods, a cannery located beside the dock.

The small boat harbor is another fixture of the downtown harbor. This marina provides more than 500 slips (docking places) for cruisers, fishing boats, and charter vessels. Nearby is the Valdez Dock Company petroleum dock, which handles refined petroleum products.

The offices and dock of the U.S. Coast Guard are also located in the downtown harbor. Using radios and radar surveillance, staff from the Coast Guard and its Vessel Traffic Service (VTS) communicate with approaching vessels and keep track of all marine traffic in port waters.

A small strip of land called Valdez Spit separates the small boat harbor from outer port waters. The emergency operations center of the Alyeska Pipeline Service Company—the firm that runs the Alyeska harbor—is located on the spit and has its own dock. This facility includes Alyeska's Ship Escort/Response Vessel System (SERVS) base. Roughly 150 SERVS workers maintain equipment and a fleet of vessels with

crews ready 24 hours a day to escort supertankers safely out of Prince William Sound. People at the SERVS base are also prepared to respond to an oil spill, should one occur. Together the Coast Guard and SERVS are the command center for the port's everyday activities and emergencies.

The Alyeska harbor across the water south of downtown centers on the product that gives Valdez its world-class status—crude oil. Unlike other harbors, the Alyeska Marine Terminal has no noisy bustle or city blocks of warehouses or swinging cranes. Instead, crude oil flows quietly and unseen through pipes into the supertankers that move in and out of the port.

If you moved to Valdez and wanted to become familiar with the port, you might take a car tour of the area. The Richardson Highway leads east out of downtown, then swings north around Duck Flats, a wildlife marsh.

*Commercial fishing vessels and pleasure boats share the small boat harbor. The harbor's facilities include a launch ramp and a boat lift that can heft 65 tons.*

◀ **Touring the Port of Valdez**

14

➤ At various times of the year, the salt marsh at Duck Flats hosts pintails, mallards, Canada geese, and other waterfowl.

A short distance from the marsh is the Port of Valdez General Cargo and Container Wharf, the biggest floating concrete dock in the world. Large, sealed air cells inside the heavy concrete make the dock light enough to float. Normally long concrete columns called pilings are sunk into the ocean floor to support such a huge dock. But the shore at this spot is too soft, and the water is too deep for pilings. Builders decided a floating dock—which could move up and down with the tide—would best serve ships.

*The General Cargo and Container Wharf, owned and operated by the City of Valdez, lies 1.5 miles east of the small boat harbor.*

Two steel causeways (roads that pass over water) connect the dock to shore, where bolts and chains anchor the causeways to the land so that the dock cannot float away. Extending 700 feet from shore, with a front end 1,200 feet wide, the dock is equipped with 13 large forklifts and with a pair of cranes that can heft up to 125 tons each. Beside the dock are 21 acres of storage space, and an additional 1,000 acres lie farther away. Nine grain silos stand near the wharf, but these are never used. The facility handles pipeline maintenance materials, logs, and fish from local canneries. Using giant cranes, dockworkers also transfer **containerized** materials from barges to trucks or from trucks to ships. Such transfer of goods from one type of vehicle to another is called **intermodal transportation.**

In the summer, large cruise ships come to the General Cargo and Container Wharf, bringing thousands of tourists from all over the world. The visitors might remain on the ship, disembark for local tours, or board buses or airplanes bound for other destinations. And because of its safe distance from a heavily populated area, this dock is the only one in Alaska that can accept shipments of military explosives. The floating dock also serves as a repair station for supertankers.

A short distance to the southeast are two privately owned docks, the Northwest Dock and the Valdez Alaska Terminal. These seldom-used facilities receive any heavy construction equipment arriving in Valdez.

Richardson Highway continues southeast across the Robe River and crosses Dayville Road, which runs westward along the port's southern shore. Buried on a steep hill along the road is a section of the Trans-Alaska Pipeline. Crude oil flowing through this part of the pipeline is on the last leg of its 800-mile journey from Prudhoe Bay on the Arctic Ocean to

> On a quiet day, hundreds of terns bask on the General Cargo and Container Wharf.

the Alyeska Marine Terminal, located a little farther west on Dayville Road.

Dayville crosses the Lowe River and runs past the Petro Star Valdez Refinery on the port's south shore. Through an agreement with Alyeska, Petro Star receives crude oil from the Trans-Alaska Pipeline. Workers refine, or process, the oil into jet or marine diesel fuel, which is trucked to the Valdez Dock Company petroleum dock in the downtown harbor and then bulk loaded (piped) into fuel barges equipped with individual tanks. Commercial airlines and the U.S. military buy the jet fuel, while both private and commercial boat operators purchase the marine fuel.

Farther west on Dayville Road, the Valdez tour stops next at the Solomon Gulch Fish Hatchery, where millions of salmon eggs incubate and hatch each year. The fry (immature) salmon are released directly into port waters.

*Workers at the Solomon Gulch Fish Hatchery raised these young salmon in indoor tanks.*

Many are later caught as adults and make up about 70 percent of the local commercial fishing catch. The haul ends up at Nautilus Foods, at one of two nearby processing plants, in floating processing ships, or sometimes at canneries in other Alaskan communities. Commercial fishing reels in profits totaling roughly $3.5 million a year for the Valdez area.

*By road the Alyeska Marine Terminal is about 14 miles from town.*

**Alyeska—Nerve Center for Alaskan Oil**

The last stop on the Valdez tour is the Alyeska Marine Terminal. The terminal covers 1,000 acres of land directly across the bay from the downtown harbor. Alyeska's facility was

*The tanker **Overseas Boston** loads up at the second of four berths (docking places) at the Alyeska harbor.*

> The electrical power plant above the Alyeska terminal generates enough energy to supply a city of 25,000 people.

completed in 1977, nine years after crude oil was first discovered in the Arctic. Each day about 1.4 million barrels (a barrel is about 42 gallons) of oil move through the Trans-Alaska Pipeline on their way to the terminal.

As oil enters the terminal, it passes through the East Metering Building at up to 84,000 barrels per hour. Each of the seven oil companies that own the crude receives a percentage of the volume. The oil is then piped either to storage tanks or directly to supertankers in port. Tankers are loaded at deepwater docks along the shore.

The facilities in the terminal include an electrical power station, meters for recording the amount of crude flowing through the pipeline, and equipment for maintaining these meters. The plant also houses its own laboratory, a heating system, a sewage system, a vapor-recovery

*Each oil storage tank at the Alyeska facility holds enough oil to fill about 38 Olympic-sized swimming pools.*

system, a water-treatment plant, a fire pump house, numerous computers and control screens, several warehouses, enormous steel oil tanks, and three tanks for storing used **ballast water.**

Designers created the terminal with efficiency and safety in mind. It sits on several terraced levels of bedrock that lead down to the harbor. Besides providing flat surfaces for buildings and equipment, the mountainside terraces also make good use of gravity by allowing oil to flow easily from storage tanks on the upper levels to loading tanks down on the shore. Because the storage tanks are elevated, they are at lower risk of damage from **tsunamis.** In addition, the highest terrace is backed by large slabs of rock that are actually bolted to the mountain to protect the terminal from mud slides and earthquakes.

Each of the 18 huge storage tanks can hold 510,000 barrels of oil. The tanks sit in pairs in nine sunken containment dikes (ditches). Should a leak or break occur, each dike is large enough to hold all the oil from both tanks, plus any snow or rain that might have collected. Instead of piling up on the tanks, snow slides off their steep, cone-shaped tops.

# DISASTER!

At 12:27 A.M. on March 24, 1989, Captain Joseph Hazelwood of the tanker *Exxon Valdez* radioed the U.S. Coast Guard in Valdez. "Yeah, it's the *Valdez* back . . . We've fetched up, ah, hard aground, north of Goose Island off Bligh Reef. And evidently, ah, leaking some oil, and, ah, you want the state notified? Over."

Within hours nearly 11 million gallons of crude oil had spilled into the waters off Bligh Reef, just south of Valdez Arm. During the next several days, winds and currents spread the oil around Prince William Sound. Although no oil reached the Port of Valdez, the town was immediately involved. Valdez became a headquarters for supplies, volunteers, Exxon workers, scientists, and assistance agencies.

Oil does not dissolve in water—it must be cleaned up. State and federal employees, private volunteers, and people from the Exxon oil company tried to get rid of the mess, using any known method—from chemicals to paper towels. In one procedure, workers on barges aimed hot water from pressure hoses to blast oil from rocks on land. In another, crews with cold-water hoses flushed the oil off the land toward boats equipped to skim the oil from the surface of the water.

Animal-rescue staff set up a center in Valdez to save as many animals as possible. Oil-covered fur and feathers can no longer insulate animals, who then die in cold weather. Eagles eat the bodies of dead seabirds, often carrying them to the nest where the oil contaminates eggs or young eagles.

The *Exxon Valdez* disaster fouled beaches and killed more birds and mammals than any other spill recorded in U.S. history. Fishing areas used by commercial fishers and Native peoples were also contaminated. The cleanup efforts were valiant, but damage was widespread and in many cases irreversible. It may be years before scientists learn the full impact of the *Exxon Valdez* accident in Prince William Sound.

The power plant and vapor-recovery system are examples of how different parts of the Alyeska terminal work together. These two facilities cooperate to protect the environment and to generate extra electricity. As crude oil sits in storage tanks, it emits invisible vapors that can pollute the air. The vapors can also burn or explode if they mix with oxygen. To prevent vapors from escaping into the atmosphere, they are piped to the power plant to fuel the boilers that make electricity. As oil leaves the storage tanks, workers reduce the risk of explosion by pumping either vapors or exhaust from the boilers into the emptying tanks so there is no room for oxygen to enter.

Alyeska also has a system in place to recycle ballast water without polluting the harbor. Ballast water is loaded onto top-heavy, empty ships to weight them so that they will not capsize. The water is removed before the vessel takes on a load. When ballast water sits in tanks that previously held oil, leftover traces of oil contaminate the ballast water. Equipment at the Alyeska terminal treats the dirty ballast water to separate out the oil. The treated water is emptied into the harbor, and the recovered oil returns to the crude oil system.

The operations control center at Alyeska keeps track of oil movement at every step. Computers monitor the entire pipeline—from Pump Station 1 at Prudhoe Bay to the terminal in Valdez. Microwave and satellite communication systems help gather information about oil flow. Workers can then study changes in flow, possible leaks, earthquake data, and any potential trouble spots within the terminal.

> ➤ The total cost of the Trans-Alaska Pipeline system, including the Alyeska Marine Terminal at Valdez, reached $8 billion upon completion in 1977. About 70,000 people worked on the project.

> ➤ Even though the Alyeska Pipeline Service Company maintains the Trans-Alaska Pipeline, the crude oil and the pipeline itself belong to seven major oil companies.

**Supertankers** ➤ Looking out across the harbor, it's easy to tell which supertankers are coming into port and which ones are leaving. Empty tankers ride high in the water, exposing the red paint on their hulls. When a tanker is loaded, its hull is underwater, and the red paint is not visible. A supertanker is a vessel that can hold 150,000 deadweight tons (dwt). Supertankers called very large crude carriers (VLCC) have a carrying capacity of 300,000 dwt. Ultra large crude carriers (ULCC) can haul more than 300,000 dwt. Because the supertankers are difficult to steer, tugboats (small, maneuverable boats with oversized engines) help conduct the enormous vessels around the port.

At the Alyeska harbor, supertankers dock at one of four berths. Three of the docks rest on pilings driven into bedrock, while the fourth floats on the water. Built in Japan and towed across the Pacific Ocean to Valdez, the floating

*A tug helps push an empty tanker through Valdez Narrows and into the port.*

berth accommodates smaller tankers of about 120,000 dwt and has an operating platform roughly 400 feet long and 96 feet wide. Oil

*At a berth in the Alyeska harbor, a tanker takes crude oil into its hold via the four loading arms* (left), *which receive the oil through a series of pipes* (below).

flows from the Alyeska facility to the ship through four 12-inch arms (loading devices) at the rate of 80,000 barrels an hour. The other three fixed platforms, each measuring 122 feet long and 96 feet wide, accommodate super-tankers ranging from 250,000 dwt to 270,000 dwt. Oil flows into these larger ships through four 16-inch arms at 100,000 barrels per hour—a bit faster here than at the floating berth. Even at these high speeds, workers can stop the flow quickly if necessary. In an emergency, it would take only about six seconds to shut off the loading arm completely.

Port workers fill about 55 tankers with crude oil each month. Normally a ship can dock, unload ballast, fill with oil, and be on its way again in less than 24 hours. Before a ship leaves the

*A pilot's boat keeps pace with the tanker that the pilot is steering out of the port. Soon the pilot will climb down a ladder off the tanker, board the boat, and return to the downtown harbor.*

dock, the tanker master (top official on the tanker) discusses navigation conditions by radio with harbor traffic monitors, including the escort tug captain, the Escort Response Vessel (ERV) captain, and the harbor pilot. If all is clear, the tanker departs from the dock with the harbor pilot on board and with the escort tug and the ERV close by. The U.S. Coast Guard tracks the tanker through Prince William Sound on its Vessel Traffic System (VTS). The harbor pilot leaves the ship at Port Etches in Hinchinbrook Entrance. Once the tanker enters the Gulf of Alaska, it is on its own.

**Keeping Tankers Safe** ➤ As tankers move in and out of the Port of Valdez, the Coast Guard constantly monitors weather conditions. Tankers are required to take extra precautions when winds reach certain speeds. For instance, winds of 30–40 knots (nautical miles per hour) mean extra tugboats

*These icebergs have split off the nearby Columbia Glacier.*

for both inbound and outbound ships. The powerful tugs help guide tankers to docks when high winds threaten to blow the huge vessels off course.

The port also monitors icebergs—the large ice chunks that break off from nearby Columbia Glacier. Sometimes when an empty tanker is heading toward Valdez Arm, the SERVS duty officer in Valdez receives a report from the Coast Guard of ice in the tanker traffic lane. A SERVS escort vessel is sent to act as an ice scout for the inbound tanker. Using lookout, radar, and searchlights (if visibility is low), the scout vessel steers about a half mile ahead of the tanker to watch for ice. Tankers have to change course when icebergs enter the traffic lanes. The SERVS vessel warns the tanker to change course if icebergs are blocking the way.

The possibility of oil leaks or spills has been a concern for Alaskans since pipeline construction began in the 1960s. That fear became a reality in 1989, when a major spill flowed into Prince William Sound and the Gulf of Alaska. Over the years, the port has put into place many safety precautions in the hopes of preventing another disaster. For example, mooring lines—cables holding the ship to the dock—are fitted with quick-release hooks. Should a serious problem occur either on the ship or on the dock, they can separate almost instantly.

Since the 1989 oil spill, the port has created additional precautions to address oil leaks or drips on the docks. When berthed at one of the docks, each tanker is surrounded by a protective containment oil boom—a rubberlike floating barrier. If a tanker should leak, the boom prevents the oil from spreading across the water. The boom remains in place during the entire process of unloading ballast and loading oil.

The two harbors in the Port of Valdez work together and serve each other, but each has different goals. The downtown harbor benefits local residents and provides a gateway into and out of Alaska. The larger Alyeska harbor plays a crucial role in filling fuel tanks throughout the United States and around the world. The two facilities are an important center of economic activity near the top of the world.

*An oil containment boom surrounds the* **Arco Fairbanks** *as it receives crude oil at Alyeska's floating berth.*

# CHAPTER TWO

# VALDEZ'S HISTORY

People have lived in modern-day Alaska for thousands of years. Scientists think that between 10,000 and 40,000 years ago, wanderers from Siberia came across a land bridge that once linked Siberia to Alaska. These immigrants' descendants are called Native Americans.

Alaska's Native peoples can be divided into three main groups—Indians, Eskimos, and Aleuts. After crossing the land bridge, Indians spread overland into central Alaska. The Eskimos and the Aleuts originally comprised a single group that came across the land bridge later and then traveled by boat to populate Alaska's coastal regions. These newcomers hunted the seals, sea otters, and walrus that lived in the area. They also were drawn by the abundance

*The Chugach Mountains surround Prince William Sound near Valdez.*

**29**

*The ancestors of these Eskimo children may have crossed the Bering land bridge in pursuit of large herds of big game animals.*

of birds and fish and harpooned their game from narrow, one-person boats called *iqyax* (similar to kayaks).

Because no written records of this period exist, no one knows precisely when humans first arrived in present-day Prince William Sound. The area's Chugach people have passed on legends of ancestors who boated from other parts of Alaska and found large glaciers covering much of the region. Although the Chugach speak a language similar to Yupik, a western Alaskan Eskimo tongue, modern Chugach elders consider themselves to be Aleuts.

Near the eastern part of the sound, archaeologists have unearthed artifacts dating back to A.D. 205. These findings, including a stone saw and slate blades, probably belonged to the sound's earliest Chugach residents. Although few ancient village sites have been found near Valdez, scientists and Chugach stories agree that the port area was used as a pathway between interior and coastal Alaska—just as it still is. The Chugach traded marine products such as skins, seal oil, and seafoods with groups in the interior. In return the Chugach received copper items and the meat and skins of caribou and moose. By the 1700s, about 700 Chugach people lived in the coastal areas of the sound.

**Europeans Arrive** ➤ Across the globe in Europe, Peter the Great, czar (ruler) of Russia, wanted to find new resource-rich lands. He hired the Danish seaman Vitus Bering to determine whether water separated North America from Siberia. In 1741 Russian

*Peter the Great never saw the results of Bering's expedition. He died only a few months after he hired Bering to explore the northern reaches of the Russian empire.*

crews under Bering became the first Europeans to explore the Gulf of Alaska. They returned with thick, valuable pelts of seals, otters, and foxes.

Meanwhile, King George III of Great Britain was seeking the Northwest Passage—a northern water route linking Europe to Asia. He sent British explorer Captain James Cook to look for the passage. Cook sailed into Prince William Sound in May 1778 and called the area Sandwich Sound, after a British nobleman. The name was later changed to Prince William Sound, in honor of George III's son.

Like the Russians, British sailors returned home with news of plentiful seals and sea otters along the coast. Rich merchants in China paid exorbitant prices for fur pelts to make warm coats, and the Russians and the British were eager to profit from this trade. They began a rush to Alaska for the "soft gold." The Russians bartered, or traded, iron tools with the Chugach in exchange for fur pelts. But the British had better and cheaper goods to offer Native people. British traders carried on a brisk business with the Chugach despite Russian efforts to keep competitors out of Alaska. Nevertheless, Russians had the greater impact on the Native population. When the Russians were friendly,

*An artist with Cook's 1778 expedition made these portraits of two Tlingit Indians who lived near Prince William Sound.*

trading with Native groups proved successful. However, some Russian ship captains raided Chugach villages, kidnapped the women, and forced the men to bring pelts as ransom for their female family members. The raids led to war, and trading sometimes stopped.

**The Spanish** ➤ The activities of the Russians and the British
**Name the Port** angered Spain, which had previously laid claim to the entire Pacific coast of North America, from Mexico north to the Arctic Ocean. By the late 1700s, news of Russian and British exploration in present-day Alaska threatened Spain's claim. In 1790 Lieutenant Salvador Fidalgo, a well-known Spanish mapmaker, boarded the *San Carlos* to lead an expedition to Prince William Sound.

Fidalgo sailed northward into the sound, giving Spanish names to various places along the way. When the waters grew shallow, Fidalgo and several crew members left the *San Carlos* in a smaller boat. Despite nasty weather, they sailed on, as Native people watched from shore.

Arriving at the northernmost head of the sound in June 1790, Fidalgo named the spot Valdes (later spelled Valdez) in honor of the minister of the Spanish navy. The small party stepped ashore, celebrated a Catholic mass, claimed the land for Spain, and then sailed away. There is no evidence that the Spanish sighted any Russian ships. But by this time, the Russians had established a settlement farther southwest on Kodiak Island. Although several other expeditions entered Prince William Sound, none stayed for thorough exploration or settlement.

> ➤ In May 1794, Lieutenant Joseph Whidbey, a British mapmaker, became one of the first European explorers to sail into the Port of Valdez.

*The Russian settlement of Sitka, about 450 miles from Prince William Sound, was an important site for fur trading.*

In the early 1800s, the Russians continued to ◄ **Furs and Fish**
build forts and settlements in what they called
"Russian America" (present-day Alaska). Trade
between the Native peoples and the Russians
took place at Nuchek, a major outpost on
Hinchinbrook Island at the eastern entrance to
the sound. Some Russians and Chugach inter-
married, and many Chugach adopted the Russian Orthodox religion. The Chugach became
dependent on Russian manufactured supplies.
Europeans also brought tobacco, alcohol, and,
unwittingly, diseases that disabled or killed
many Native people. By 1880 the Native population had dropped to 264.

Meanwhile, news of Russian America's natural wealth traveled south to the United States. In the mid-1800s, droves of U.S. citizens headed north on whalers and fishing boats. They also came by land in the hopes of finding gold and other minerals. In 1867 Russia sold Russian America to the United States for $7.2 million. The United States called the territory Alaska, after the region's Aleut name, Alyeska, which means "great land" or "mainland."

By the end of the 1800s, Alaska's otter, seal, and walrus populations had declined from overhunting. The abundance of salmon in the

*Salmon, near the end of their life cycle, return to lay eggs in the creek near Valdez where they were hatched.*

Prince William Sound area, however, spurred a new industry—fish canning. Businesspeople in U.S. cities such as Seattle, Washington, and San Francisco, California, built canneries in Alaska. The shift from fur to fish brought population changes, too. Native peoples and newcomers moved from far-flung Alaskan trading posts to settle near canneries around the sound.

But neither fur nor salmon caused the most dramatic growth in the present-day Valdez area. In 1896 the shout of "Gold!" echoed near the Klondike River in the Yukon and sent a ripple of excitement around the world. Prospectors, nicknamed stampeders, piled onto ships and raced to the Klondike to stake their claims.

Most stampeders landed at the Alaskan towns of Skagway and St. Michael and then trekked overland or boated to the goldfields. The trails were long and difficult, and the prospectors yearned for a quicker, easier route.

The superintendent of the Pacific Steam Whaling Company, which ran four Alaskan canneries, had an idea. Why send empty ships from San Francisco and Seattle to Alaska to pick up canned fish? Why not make money by offering transportation on the ships to the stampeders? In the hopes of attracting passengers, the company spread a rumor that an easy trail over Valdez Glacier led to the riches of the Klondike.

Roughly 200 stampeders bought tickets on Pacific Steam Whaling Company vessels headed to Prince William Sound. Upon arrival the prospectors found themselves on a muddy beach in the wilderness, gazing at the distant Valdez Glacier. With no easy trail over the glacier, they were stranded. In 1897 and 1898, some 3,500 more men and women followed.

The Valdez route to the Klondike was no picnic. Most stampeders were *cheechakos* (a word meaning newcomers, derived from western North American Indian languages). The cheechakos faced steep slopes, glaciers, avalanches, and blizzards. Lacking proper clothing and equipment, the newcomers suffered frostbite, snow blindness, scurvy, fatigue, and despair. They ate their food raw or half-cooked. Many died, and many turned back. A few straggled through to the goldfields.

A U.S. Army expedition came to the stampeders' aid. Soldiers cared for the sick and gave jobs to those who did not continue the trip. In September 1899, another army expedition cleared a rough track through Keystone Canyon, east of Valdez, and explored farther into central Alaska. With the new path, the

*A group of stampeders* (facing page), *among those stubborn or lucky enough to reach the Klondike, pose in front of a rough cabin on their claim.*

route to Alaska's interior, and therefore to the Klondike, became more accessible.

Mineral wealth was soon unearthed in Alaska, too. Nome on the Bering Sea and Fairbanks in the interior saw gold rushes of their own. Oil and coal were discovered east of Valdez in the Wrangell Mountains. In the late 1890s, two prospectors found deposits of copper at Landlocked Bay near the eastern entrance to Valdez Arm. Other deposits were soon uncovered nearby. The Ellamar Copper Mine, 20 miles southwest of Valdez, opened in 1900 and became one of the region's top five copper mines. Soon afterward the Cliff Gold Mine started operating 10 miles from Valdez.

The town and port of Valdez were born partly because of the Klondike gold rush. Stampeders who could not face traveling over Valdez Glacier built homes on the silty deposits at the base of the glacier. Stores, streets, and houses sprang up along the shoreline. By 1900 about 315 people were living in Valdez.

At the beginning of the 1900s, Captain William Abercrombie of the U.S. Army played a large role in developing Valdez. First he set up Fort Liscum on the southern side of the port

◄ **Connecting with Interior Alaska**

*Fort Liscum*

*Captain William Abercrombie*

➤ President Theodore Roosevelt established Chugach National Forest on July 23, 1907. The forest lies on the shores of Prince William Sound.

➤ Major Wilds Preston Richardson, who served in the U.S. Army in the 1910s, helped transform a trail passable only by dogsled to the 400-mile, paved, all-weather Richardson Highway that bears his name.

and used the fort as his headquarters. Then he hired some of the townspeople to help build a road from Valdez north to Fairbanks. This road would later become the Richardson Highway. Bypassing Valdez Glacier along an old Chugach footpath, Abercrombie and his crews cut, sawed, hacked, and blasted their way through Keystone Canyon and Thompson Pass east of Valdez. Workers also mapped the area and collected scientific information about birds, plants, and geology.

Communication improved, too, with the Washington-Alaska Military Cable and Telegraph System. The 3,728-mile line, finished in 1902, connected Nome to Valdez overland and Valdez to Seattle by submarine cable. The new system allowed people in Valdez to communicate with the continental United States, and thus with the rest of the world. Valdez had developed into a link to and a supply center for interior Alaska.

Although the population declined somewhat as people left after the gold rush, Valdez still served as a mining and transportation center for interior Alaska. From Valdez workers shipped fox pelts to St. Louis, Missouri; Paris, France; and London, England. Copper and gold went to Tacoma, Washington. Lumber for construction projects arrived from Seattle. Tourists embarked on sightseeing trips around the sound and took launches from Valdez to Portage Pass on the western edge of the sound, where they continued to Anchorage.

In the next decades, the Port of Valdez grew slowly and steadily. In the 1920s and 1930s, the Alaska Steamship Company provided transportation and mail service to and from the town. Ships heading north from the continental United States to Valdez brought new automobiles, food, mining supplies, lumber, mail, and passengers. Ships heading out of the port carried furs, clams, crabs, herring, salmon, and more passengers.

Because of its strategic location near the Pacific Ocean, Valdez became crucial to the U.S. military when the United States entered World War II in 1941. A series of military posts stretched from Valdez to the Alaskan interior. Soldiers and thousands of tons of supplies traveled through the port and over the Richardson Highway to and from the posts. The port also became a transfer point for materials used in

➤ In 1912 the U.S. Congress approved funding for additional navigational lights near Valdez. A few months later, a full cargo of new lights was lost in a shipwreck near the entrance to Prince William Sound.

➤ Businessman Owen Meals brought Valdez's first open-cockpit airplane, *Spirit of Valdez*, to town by boat in 1927. Soon pilots began making trips to central Alaska—a journey of three days by automobile but only two hours by airplane.

*Travelers cross a stretch of the Alaska Highway that runs through Canada's Yukon Territory.*

building the Alaska Highway, which runs northward from Dawson Creek, British Columbia, to Delta Junction, Alaska. Constructed as an overland military supply route, the road, finished in 1942, linked Valdez to Canada and to the continental United States.

In the years after World War II, Alaskans wanted their territory to become a state. Late in

1946, Alaskan citizens voted to request statehood, and most people in the continental United States supported the idea. By 1955 Alaskan officials had written a state constitution for Alaska. On January 3, 1959, President Dwight D. Eisenhower admitted Alaska into the Union as the forty-ninth state.

Around the time of statehood, Valdez maintained a steady business exporting fish from local canneries to the continental United States. The port's progress was interrupted on March 27, 1964, when a huge earthquake ripped through the southern central part of Alaska. Huge tsunami waves washed away Valdez's dock, drowning 32 people. After the quake, the town was condemned because of its unsafe site. Citizens of Valdez moved and rebuilt their town five miles to the west, away from the unstable ground at the foot of Valdez Glacier.

*Little remains of Old Valdez* (above) *except some dock pilings and debris on the beach. The rebuilt city is visible in the distance. The 1964 tsunami washed away the dock and much of the town* (facing page).

# THE DAY THE EARTH SHOOK

The 400-foot steamship *Chena* docked at Valdez on March 27, 1964, a peaceful Friday afternoon. Workers unloaded supplies and gave oranges to children watching on the pier, which extended far out into deep water. The town lay behind the dock, unaware of the tragedy to come.

The earthquake gave little warning. Suddenly the ground cracked open and geysers—spurts of hot underground water—shot 10 feet into the air. The dock, and everyone on it, sank in an underwater landslide, swallowed up by the quivering sand along the beach. A huge water wave—a tsunami—rushed in, washing over the waterfront and into town. Fuel tanks on shore broke and burst into flames. Stunned townspeople ran for high ground. During the evening, additional tremors sent more large waves rolling into Valdez. The waterfront and much of the town lay in ruins. Thirty-two people died.

When the quake was over, the U.S. government condemned the Valdez site, forcing the townspeople to relocate. Residents chose more stable ground five miles to the west.

The 1964 earthquake was a wake-up call. It alerted builders to design structures to withstand the trauma caused by earthquakes and strong waves. In 1977 when the Alyeska Marine Terminal was completed across the bay from town, the facility included several safety features. For instance, the oil storage tanks were placed on the uppermost terrace of the terminal site. There the tanks would be out of reach of a tsunami like the one that swept into Old Valdez in 1964.

In 1968 scientists discovered crude oil in Prudhoe Bay on the North Slope. Prospectors esti-
mated that they could remove 9.6 billion
barrels of oil from the site. At the time of the
discovery, the United States and many Euro-
pean nations were importing large amounts of
oil, mainly from a trade bloc of oil-rich nations
known as the Organization of Petroleum Exporting Countries (OPEC). In the 1970s, OPEC
raised its oil prices and refused to sell oil to
countries that did not support OPEC's political
views. The resulting oil shortage led U.S. petroleum companies to develop more oil and gas
fields at home. In 1973 the federal government
placed a ban on the sale of oil from the North
Slope to foreign markets. The restriction, aimed
at reducing U.S. dependence on foreign oil, re-
mained in place for 23 years.

In 1974 construction began on a pipeline to
transport oil from Prudhoe Bay to Alaska's
southern coast. From there the oil could be

*A welder joins two sections of pipe for the Trans-Alaska Pipeline* (facing page). *Upon the pipeline's completion, news reporters and Alyeska employees near Pump Station 1 at Prudhoe Bay listen for the sounds of the very first flow of North Slope oil through the pipe* (right).

> Prudhoe Bay is the world's twelfth largest oil field and the biggest ever discovered in North America.

shipped to the rest of the United States. Developers chose the Port of Valdez as the end point of the pipeline because of the port's deepwater harbor and year-round, ice-free status. When oil began flowing through the 800-mile Trans-Alaska Pipeline in 1977, the economy in Valdez boomed.

The town and the port buzzed with activity in preparation for servicing the pipeline and the huge oil tankers. The U.S. Coast Guard established its first Marine Safety Office. The port beefed up its radio communications equipment and added more navigational aids and radar systems at Valdez Narrows and along Valdez Arm. The federal government sent ships to rechart the tanker route into and out of the port. The huge Alyeska Marine Terminal was the biggest project of all. The town's population—about 1,000 people at the census of 1970—tripled as newcomers arrived to work at construction jobs. A three-year project, the terminal was finished in 1977.

*In designing the Trans-Alaska Pipeline, engineers considered factors such as permafrost (frozen ground), earthquakes, wildlife, and visual effect. The pipeline has a zigzag design that absorbs ground movement and weather changes and allows the pipe to expand and contract.*

The first supertanker to fill up at the Alyeska terminal was the *Arco Juneau*, which left the port on August 1, 1977, bound for the U.S. West Coast. The oil in the *Juneau's* hold was worth $7.2 million—the exact price for which Russia sold Alaska to the United States in 1867.

Oil prices climbed steadily in the late 1970s, a period when the Trans-Alaska Pipeline carried close to its top capacity of 2.2 million barrels a day. In response to high costs, consumers used less and less oil. Prices peaked in 1981 and then fell suddenly as too much oil flooded the market. In the summer of 1986, oil prices plunged to their lowest point ever, and oil companies scaled back on production in an effort to bolster the industry. In 1989 the oil industry weathered widespread criticism of the *Exxon Valdez* spill. Since then oil prices have stabilized but remain flat.

**Exxon Valdez** *cleanup crews spray hot water from a barge onto oil-fouled rocks in Prince William Sound.*

➤ Outsiders rushing in to help with the 1989 *Exxon Valdez* oil spill tripled the city's population almost overnight. People soon ran out of places to stay. Some said only living room couches were left, and those were renting for $100 a night!

The changing fortunes of the oil business do not affect Valdez directly. But the companies' profits supply the tax dollars that fuel the town's economy. Oil firms and the state of Alaska have agreed that, as less and less oil is available for extraction, oil companies should pay less tax money each year. This arrangement has cut into the amount of money that Valdez receives for its annual budget. Town officials are looking into ways to help make up the shortfall.

In 1996, after a review of national interests, the U.S. government decided to lift the ban on foreign oil sales and to allow the sale of North Slope oil to both U.S. and international markets. For two decades, all oil that flowed from the North Slope through Valdez had gone by law only to U.S. markets on the West Coast, in the U.S. Virgin Islands, and on the Gulf of Mexico.

Also in 1996, Valdez officials noted that the downtown harbor, like many Alaskan harbors, needs repairs and upgrades. Docks and other facilities that were built in the mid-1960s have deteriorated or become outmoded. Authorities must decide how and when to complete the work so that Valdez Harbor will maintain its role in the town's, and the state's, economy into the next century.

Valdez has experienced triumphs and disasters over the centuries—from its early days as a Chugach footpath to its modern status as a major oil port. Profits from the sale of crude oil help keep Valdez prosperous. Tourism is strong and continues to grow. Developers want to build a gas pipeline alongside the Trans-Alaska Pipeline to tap into some 26 trillion cubic feet of natural gas that lie in the oil fields at Prudhoe Bay. Such a project would mean more expansion and activity. The future for the Port of Valdez seems bright.

*Port officials plan to replace floats, the water system, and the electrical system in the small boat harbor within five years.*

# CHAPTER THREE

# VALDEZ AT WORK

*The second mate, or third-highest official, of the* **Arco Juneau** *checks a water line on board the ship.*

People and nations of the world trade with one another for a variety of reasons. A country might have the resources and skills to produce some products for export. The same nation may import other goods it lacks. Trade allows citizens to enjoy products they could not otherwise obtain and enables a country to use its workers, natural resources, and money in the most productive way. The state of Alaska, for instance, has an abundance of fish and seafood. About 90 percent of Alaska's seafood exports go to Japan. Alaska, in turn, imports steel from Japan. This trading between Alaska and Japan is an example of international trade, while trading within a country's own borders is called domestic trade.

The difference between the value of a country's imports and the value of its exports is called the **balance of trade**. When a nation exports more goods and services than it imports, that nation is said to have a positive balance of trade or a trade surplus. A country with more imports than exports has a negative balance of trade or a trade deficit. In the past, many governments felt that trade surpluses were of utmost importance to national wealth and could only be attained by throwing other countries into trade deficits.

To achieve and maintain trade surpluses, most countries practiced **protectionism** in their international trade policies. To protect domestic enterprises, governments imposed tariffs (fees on imports) and quotas (limits on the amount of goods that can enter a country) to increase the prices of foreign goods. These higher prices encouraged a nation's consumers to buy less expensive, locally made products. Governments reasoned that such purchases protected the jobs of that country's workers.

But many people began arguing that trade surpluses and protectionism are not necessary. Supporters of free trade believe that if goods flow freely through ports, consumers will buy more and national economies will grow. In addition, the purchase of foreign goods provides money to foreign markets, allowing foreign consumers to buy more imported goods. For example, when Americans purchase Mexican agricultural products, then Mexicans have money to buy American-made cars.

In keeping with this idea, many groups of countries have formed free trade agreements—

> Alaska is the only U.S. state that exports more goods than it imports.

pacts in which nations agree to reduce or remove their protectionist policies when trading with one another. In 1994 the United States, Canada, and Mexico entered into the **North American Free Trade Agreement (NAFTA).** According to the agreement, the three countries became a single market. A number of trade restrictions were dropped immediately, and the rest were scheduled for elimination within the next 15 years. Many people feared that NAFTA would result in the loss of jobs for American workers. But NAFTA has created as many American jobs as it has lost, and trade among the three member nations has increased since the treaty took effect.

Like the members of NAFTA, many countries have lowered trade restrictions in the 1990s. In addition to trade agreements, the 1990s ushered in other kinds of cooperation among nations. Former Communist countries (with government-controlled economies) and capitalist countries (with privately run marketplaces) have formed friendlier relations than they once had. For example, Russia welcomes technological and financial help from U.S. oil companies to develop Russian oil deposits.

**North Slope Oil** ➤ Centrally located between the markets of Europe, northeastern Asia, and North America, Valdez is an ideal transfer hub. The port's position along the Pacific Rim (a group of wealthy countries bordering the Pacific Ocean) allows convenient exporting to Japan, South Korea, and Canada—Alaska's top three foreign markets.

Valdez's primary product is crude oil. In fact, 80 percent of the port's business is oil exports.

When the Trans-Alaska Pipeline was completed in 1977, oil from Prudhoe Bay provided 25 percent of all U.S.-produced crude oil for U.S. markets. Until 1996 every drop of oil that passed through Valdez was slated for domestic, not international, markets. The end of the export ban meant that North Slope crude oil could be sold to nations such as Japan, South Korea, and Taiwan. At first some U.S. unionized workers fought against lifting the ban. They feared the action might open jobs to foreign workers on foreign ships, leaving less opportunity for union members. But in fact, 11,000 more jobs became available for Americans. Exported oil travels on U.S. vessels with American crews, and the ships submit to yearly inspection by the U.S. Coast Guard.

In the mid-1990s, Alaska supplied 20 percent of total U.S. crude oil production. Despite the fall of the crude oil export ban, about 92 percent of Alaska's oil still goes to domestic markets on the U.S. West Coast. Another 5 percent travels to Asia. Only about 3 percent of North Slope oil stays in Alaska.

➤ Alaskans sometimes call oil "black gold" because of the wealth it has brought to the state.

➤ Each day South Korea receives about 30,000 barrels of crude from Valdez. Alaskan oil sales to South Korea total roughly $240 million a year.

**Oil's Role at Home** ➤ In many ways, crude oil is the lifeblood of the Alaskan and Valdezan economies. Five of the state's top ten private companies employ workers in the oil and gas industries, which account for 40 percent of all the jobs in Alaska. Oil is the livelihood of many Valdezans, too. Although Alyeska employs just under 20 percent of the Valdez workforce, many more jobs—in transportation and health services, for example—support the oil industry indirectly.

Alaska produces more oil than it uses and exports its excess crude oil through the Port of Valdez. When oil prices go up around the world, Alaska sells its oil for a bigger profit, and the state benefits. For instance, depending on production levels, a $1 increase for each barrel of oil can add an extra $100 million to the state treasury. Alaska also collects royalties (shares of profits), taxes, and leasing fees from petroleum companies for the oil and gas drilled from the state's deposits.

*The Trans-Alaska Pipeline* (facing page) *carries crude oil drilled from land or from offshore rigs* (below) *at Prudhoe Bay.*

# THE CRUDE OIL JOURNEY

Crude oil makes a long, complex journey from an underground deposit to the fuel tank of a school bus. Drills at Prudhoe Bay tap into the oil thousands of feet beneath the ground—or even beneath the bay itself. Pumps move the crude to the Trans-Alaska Pipeline, through which the oil makes the 800-mile trip south to Valdez.

And what a trip it is! The pipeline runs underground in some areas and above ground in others. The route crosses three mountain ranges—the Brooks, the Alaska, and the Chugach. The oil in the pipe passes through many weather systems with temperatures varying from

−80° F to 95° F, depending on the time of year and the local climate. The pipeline crosses rivers and streams more than 800 times during the trip. As many as 11 pump stations keep the oil flowing along its way south at a rate of five miles per hour. It takes a week for a single barrel of oil to reach Valdez.

When the oil reaches the Alyeska terminal at Valdez, it goes through the metering building for measurement. The oil is then stored in Alyeska's tanks, ready to be pumped into the hold of a supertanker at one of the four terminal docks. Once loaded, the tankers head to refineries around the world—to U.S. destinations such as Hawaii and California or to international destinations such as South Korea and Taiwan. Refinery workers process crude oil into automobile and aviation fuel, as well as into heating oil and other petroleum products. Consumers and businesses buy the fuels to warm their homes or to run their cars, trucks, airplanes, and school buses.

Nearly 85 percent of the funding for state government comes from taxes and royalties on oil. The money enables the state to build and maintain roads, schools, hospitals, and other facilities that serve the people of Valdez and other Alaskan towns. Oil companies do not always agree with the state about how much they should pay for using Alaska's land and water. The businesses want the state to reduce use taxes so they can spend more on exploring and developing new fields. But the Alaskan government wants to collect more taxes and royalties to provide more services and to improve the quality of life for the state's residents.

Because so much oil money supports the state, Alaskans enjoy benefits that the citizens of many other states do not. For instance, Alaskans do not pay a state income tax. And since the early 1980s, a permanent fund dividend—a savings account set up by the state to invest oil money—has paid an allotted yearly amount to each Alaskan (including children) who has lived in the state for at least one year. In the late 1990s, the amount was close to $1,000.

Valdez city officials realize that the oil-driven money surplus might not last forever. So like the state government, they have set up several investment funds for the city. The funds are similar to savings accounts to be used for a "rainy day."

**Future Prospects, ➤ Hard Decisions**

In the decades since drillers discovered oil at Prudhoe Bay, oil companies have adjusted their original estimate of how much crude they can extract from the reserves. In 1997 scientists predicted that nearly 13 billion barrels could be removed from Prudhoe Bay and that the deposit would last another 20 years or more. New discoveries could extend the forecast even farther.

Even so, Alaska faces some tough decisions about oil. Oil supplies from current drilling sites are limited, and global trade patterns shift over time. For example, in the late 1980s, the United States began to increase its oil imports as production fell and consumption rose. During the mid-1990s, imports supplied slightly more than half the country's needs. In addition, U.S. oil companies, developers, and many workers are concerned about competition from Pacific Rim nations such as Russia and China, which are developing their own oil fields. The fear is that Alaska and the United States will be left behind in the world market if new sources of oil and gas are not developed at home.

Since the export ban was lifted and new markets have opened up for Alaskan oil, many companies are pushing for further development. They want permission to explore and to build on potential fields in undeveloped areas. In 1996 Alaska's governor approved construction of the Northstar oil drilling site, located six miles north of Prudhoe Bay in the Beaufort Sea. Once the Northstar project is completed, the oil will flow through the Trans-Alaska Pipeline to the Port of Valdez, increasing oil profits and assuring the port of a continued source of business.

The oil industry is also interested in the Arctic National Wildlife Refuge (ANWR). Some 9.2 billion barrels of oil lie under the coastal plain of this large, federally protected wilderness area, 65 miles east of Prudhoe Bay. Oil interests argue

*The pig, made of several hundred pounds of plastic, is used to clean the pipeline.*

➤ Crude oil turns waxy when it touches the inside of the pipe. To clean off the build-up, workers send a mechanical device called a pig through the pipeline. The flow of oil pushes the pig through the pipe, scraping the wax off the pipe and mixing it back into the oil.

that the site could provide jobs and revenue, thus securing Alaska's economic future. The oil would also bring more business to the Port of Valdez. Petroleum companies are pressuring the federal government to open a portion of ANWR for exploration and development.

But the idea of oil expansion in ANWR is unpopular with many people. The bulk of ANWR oil would be slated for export to Japan—a result that would not solve the U.S. problem of dependence on foreign oil. In addition, the refuge is a sanctuary for caribou, polar bears, musk oxen, and about 200 other kinds of Arctic animals. Many Native people in the area rely on the caribou for food and clothing. Environmentalists say that preserving Alaska's wilderness and the lifeways of its Native peoples is more important than the jobs and profits that drilling in the ANWR would create.

*More than 19 million acres of pristine wilderness conceal vast amounts of crude oil in the Arctic National Wildlife Refuge, established in 1960.*

All year round, the downtown harbor of the Port of Valdez handles a variety of general cargo (packaged goods). Imports comprise about 15 percent of the port's business. Many of these goods are packed in huge steel containers and shipped by barge to Valdez. Modular housing, consisting of ready-made sections such as walls and roofs, is one kind of containerized cargo that moves through Valdez. At the Port of Valdez General Cargo and Container Wharf, workers use cranes to transfer the containers to trucks. The trucks deliver the parts to construction sites in central Alaska, where builders can quickly assemble the house. For products such as modular houses, Valdez is truly the Gateway to the Interior.

Logs from Alaska's interior forests travel in the opposite direction. They arrive in Valdez by truck, where laborers load them onto barges in the harbor. From the port, the barges head south to British Columbia, to Washington, or to Oregon for processing into lumber or pulp. In 1996 Valdez exported more than 228,000 short tons of logs.

➤ Container traffic is measured in twenty-foot equivalent units (TEUs). One TEU represents a container that is 20 feet long, 8 feet wide, and 8.5 feet or 9.5 feet high.

➤ In 1994 Alaska sold almost 663,000 tons of wood products worth nearly $510 million to foreign markets in Asia and Europe, as well as to Egypt and Canada.

*Piles of logs await export and recently imported containerized goods lie in stacks while a cruise ship floats at the General Cargo and Container Wharf.*

*Two fishermen supervise as a crane hauls a cargo of freshly caught salmon out of the hold of the boat.*

> In the mid-1990s, Alaska exported well over $1 billion a year in seafood products.

> In 1994 the fish and shellfish caught in Alaskan waters amounted to more than half of all the seafood harvested in the United States.

Fish is another important export from the Port of Valdez. Fish and log exports combined make up 5 percent of the port's business. In the mid-1990s, Alaska annually harvested nearly 3 million tons of seafood—including groundfish, herring, halibut, shellfish, and salmon. While seafood from other parts of the state is exported to Japan, Valdez sends its seafood products to commercial plants along the West Coast of the United States. From these plants, the food goes to domestic or foreign distributors. Most of the fish shipped or processed in the Valdez area is salmon. Catches end up at one of three facilities near Valdez or at a floating processing plant—a ship outfitted to prepare seafood for consumption. Workers clean the fish and then can, freeze, or package it fresh right on board the vessel. The floating processing plant holds the fish until it can be loaded onto another ship and then taken to markets in Japan or on the West Coast.

The Port of Valdez provides several specialty services. The General Cargo and Container Wharf handles weapons and explosives sent to and from Alaskan military bases. The U.S. Coast Guard oversees the movement of military goods through Valdez. Coast Guard workers make sure that shippers have the proper explosive permits and that the items are stored correctly. Most of the explosives and munitions brought to Alaska come by barge from the Naval Weapons Station in Concord, California, in boxcar-sized containers. Cranes carefully lift the containers from the barges and place them on trucks. Once the transfer is complete, vehicles take the munitions to bases in Fairbanks or Anchorage, or to other Alaskan military installations. Any unused weapons and ammunition are shipped back to California.

Valdez is a **foreign trade zone (FTZ).** International manufacturers can store or alter (paint, for example) goods in an FTZ without paying local taxes or U.S. import duties. This arrangement makes it cheaper for overseas companies to export goods to the United States. Valdez city officials have set aside several pieces of land at the airport and along the waterfront for FTZ use. These plots are available to businesses from other countries for storage or processing.

The FTZ designation makes Valdez more attractive to a variety of companies and represents another source of income for the port. Whether or not new oil fields are developed in Alaska, the supply of petroleum will run out someday. As Alaskan oil is depleted over the years, the alternative forms of business that the FTZ can bring will become more important to Valdez.

*A tug escorts a tanker into the port. With skillful management of oil resources, the Port of Valdez will be busy for a long time to come.*

Specialty facilities, containerized traffic, and other non-oil cargoes are all part of Valdez's on-going effort to diversify port services. Much of the port's activity relies upon oil, and Valdez's prosperity depends on oil industries at home and abroad. A wider range of income sources will help guarantee Valdez's economic future in a rapidly changing world market.

# CHAPTER FOUR

# SMALL TOWN, BIG BUSINESS

Small Town, Big Business—that describes Valdez in a nutshell. Billions of dollars' worth of crude oil flow through a town of just 4,500 people. Yet for all its economic impact on Valdez, the oil is never seen, heard, or smelled as it goes from pipeline to storage tanks to supertankers. Because this principal commodity is out of sight, it might be easy to forget that one-fifth of all U.S. oil travels through Valdez. That's big business.

This modern, well-planned town lies at the foot of glacier-capped peaks alongside waterways rich with fish, animals, and birds. Valdez is known by a couple of nicknames—Gateway to the Interior, for its geographic relation to the rest of Alaska, and Little Switzerland, because of

*Light traffic moves along a Valdez street against a backdrop of mountains.*

*The majestic Chugach Mountains rise in jagged peaks around the shores of Valdez Arm.*

the town's spectacular mountain scenery. Many people who visit the small town are reminded of pretty villages in the Swiss Alps.

Unlike the weather in Switzerland, however, the climate in Valdez can be dreary. About 60 inches of rain fall each year. And in winter, short days and heavy snow can make it hard for Valdezans to keep their spirits up. But on a clear, sunny day, residents and tourists alike are amazed at the breathtaking beauty of the town's setting.

**◄ Small-Town Friendliness**

Valdez has many advantages of small-town life. Most residents know one another and exchange friendly waves as they pass on the streets. There are no stoplights in town. Crime rates are low—in one five-year period, there

After leaving Prince William Sound, a plane flying due south from Valdez would not reach land until it got to Tuamotu, an island group near Tahiti in the South Pacific—more than 5,000 miles away.

were only two murders, two robberies, and five cases of arson in Valdez. Police arrests are usually limited to incidents such as theft and traffic violations.

Valdez has two radio stations and two weekly newspapers. Although there is no movie theater in town, popular movies are shown on weekends at the large civic center. For people interested in history, the Valdez Museum contains all kinds of artifacts and photographs that help tell the town's story. Valdezans have an answer to the fact that the town has no art gallery—"Our pipeline is a work of art. It is the world's largest steel sculpture."

The Prince William Sound area is home to several Native villages, and about 250 Native people, including Chugach and other groups, live and work in Valdez. They represent about 5 percent of the town's population. The majority of Valdezans—90 percent—are Caucasian. Other ethnic groups, such as Asian-Americans and African-Americans, make up the remaining 5 percent.

*The Valdez Civic and Convention Center contains meeting rooms and performance space for a variety of events each year.*

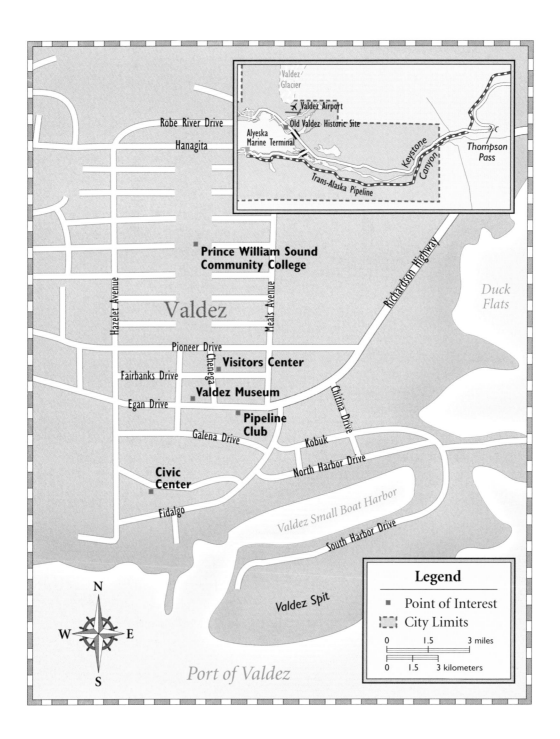

Robe River Drive

Hanagita

Valdez Glacier

✈ Valdez Airport

Old Valdez Historic Site

Alyeska Marine Terminal

Trans-Alaska Pipeline

Keystone Canyon

Thompson Pass

Prince William Sound Community College

Hazelet Avenue

Meals Avenue

Valdez

Richardson Highway

Duck Flats

Pioneer Drive

Chenega

Visitors Center

Fairbanks Drive

Chitina Drive

Valdez Museum

Egan Drive

Pipeline Club

Galena Drive

Kobuk

Civic Center

North Harbor Drive

Fidalgo

Valdez Small Boat Harbor

South Harbor Drive

N
W E
S

Valdez Spit

**Legend**

■ Point of Interest

City Limits

0    1.5    3 miles

0    1.5    3 kilometers

Port of Valdez

*A sailor on board the* Arco Juneau *stands on watch at the ship's bow (front).*

In addition to its permanent population, Valdez also has a transient group of citizens whom the locals don't often see. They work on tankers, tugboats, and escort vessels and might be out on the water for months at a time, spending only a few hours or days in town. Some of these workers make their homes in other parts of the United States and fly back during their free time. According to the quarterly publication *Alaska Geographic,* "[These people] know Valdez from the shoreline out and from the airport up." On the other hand, some Valdezan vessel workers are employed in other U.S. ports and fly home for breaks or vacations.

**A Prosperous Community** ➤ Because oil is the mainstay of Valdez, it is not surprising that private oil companies hire the greatest number of residents. The Alyeska terminal alone employs more than 270 people. Alyeska encourages its employees to live in Valdez and to become part of the community. Another 150 people work for SERVS, the supertanker escort and emergency team that directly supports the oil industry. An additional 200 people work in transportation jobs that are related to oil production and trade. Among them are some 20 members of the Southwest Alaska Pilots Association, who steer tankers in and out of the Alyeska terminal. These pilots also handle the cruise ships that stop at the floating concrete dock in the summertime. About 50 U.S. Coast Guard officers oversee all aspects of marine transportation in Valdez.

*Two civic center employees, members of Valdez's service sector, greet visitors with friendly smiles.*

Service jobs—positions that provide services rather than goods—make up more than 80 percent of the Valdez economy. The service sector includes not only pipeline-related employees but also workers in government, health services, transportation, retail, and education. Local, state, and federal government jobs account for about 27 percent of the Valdez service workforce. Some health-care providers work at the city-owned Valdez Community Hospital. About 25 laborers from the North Star Terminal and

> It would take 14 times the population of Valdez to fill the Rose Bowl stadium in Pasadena, California. Yet Valdez is the ninth largest city in Alaska, which has just 600,000 people.

Stevedore Company do much of the work of receiving, discharging, and loading vessels and trucks at the General Cargo and Container Wharf. Many Valdezans hold retail and hospitality jobs, providing services for tourists in hotels, restaurants, gift shops, and camping-supply stores. Valdez doesn't have many clothing stores—residents and tourists do that kind of shopping in Anchorage or in other large cities. For the most part, residents live a casual lifestyle, and they dress to match. Diners at the expensive Pipeline Club are welcome whether they wear a T-shirt or a tie.

Outside the service sector, about 13 percent of Valdezans work in manufacturing—processing raw materials into goods for sale. In the Valdez area, fish processing, oil refining, and the timber industry comprise the bulk of manufacturing jobs. Construction employs about 4 percent of the labor force. Workers make roads, erect buildings, and help maintain the pipeline. Mining and agriculture combined provide jobs for only 3 percent of Valdezans.

*College students work part-time cleaning salmon on a fish cannery "slime line."*

Most Valdez workers bring home a substantial salary. Jobs in the oil industry pay well—the average family income in Valdez is about $70,000 a year. Only about 200 people live below the poverty level. The healthy economy shows in several ways. Impressive homes line the wide, paved streets of Valdez's residential section, where houses become grander the farther away from the waterfront. Many homes have several vehicles parked outside—RVs, vans, and large trucks—not to mention snowmobiles and motorized watercraft. Some families keep pleasure boats in the town's small boat harbor. A few Valdez residents own second homes in other parts of the country.

The prosperous economy also contributes to Valdez's good schools. Nearly 1,000 students attend the three schools in Valdez, from kindergarten through high school. After high school, many students in the area go to Prince William Sound Community College, located on the north end of town. The community college is affiliated with the University of Alaska at Anchorage.

Besides paying good wages, private oil companies support Valdez's economy by paying property taxes. Because of the oil industry, Valdez has one of the highest municipal tax bases in Alaska. Property taxes from the Alyeska Marine Terminal make up 92 percent of the city's tax dollars. These taxes, in turn, fund two-thirds of the city's total budget. Local government officials use the money for basic services—such as roads, fire stations, and police protection—and to make life more enjoyable for Valdezans. For example, people in town enjoy fine public facilities, such as a

*A distinctive wooden sculpture marks student housing at Prince William Sound Community College.*

*The tour boat* MV Glacier Queen II *(facing page) carries sightseers past Columbia Glacier for a close-up look.*

large civic center, a modern and well-stocked library, and a teen center. The federal and state governments, with help from city volunteers, maintain beautiful wilderness trails for recreation. Valdezans even have a four-field softball complex specially designed to drain melting snow quickly for spring ball games.

Although the city is financially healthy, oil profits—like profits in most industries—rise and fall. Alaskan oil profits have declined since the late 1980s. This decrease has forced city officials to find other ways to fund some of the benefits provided to residents. For instance, the local swimming pool has begun to collect fees to help offset the loss of oil income.

**Having Fun in Valdez** 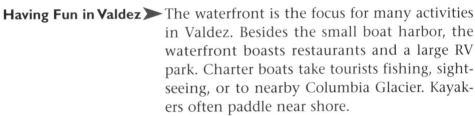 The waterfront is the focus for many activities in Valdez. Besides the small boat harbor, the waterfront boasts restaurants and a large RV park. Charter boats take tourists fishing, sightseeing, or to nearby Columbia Glacier. Kayakers often paddle near shore.

Cruise ships with passengers from all over the world find their way to Valdez. Roughly 68,000 cruise ship passengers stop in Valdez each year, and about half of them disembark. Passengers step off the floating concrete dock outside Valdez and onto buses that make the short run to town. It is not unusual to hear a variety of foreign languages as tourists pass on the street.

Residents and visitors enjoy the surrounding wilderness in many ways. People take scenic hikes from the tree-lined shore upward through spruce forests to alpine meadows blanketed with wildflowers. Hunters pursue bears or Dall sheep. Photographers aim their cameras at the

> Because of the prosperous oil economy, teachers in Valdez earn higher salaries than in many other U.S. cities.

sky in search of Canada geese and trumpeter swans or at the water for glimpses of whales and harbor seals. Fishing enthusiasts can catch halibut, salmon, and crab or scour the beaches for a harvest of clams. Tourists receive a good return on their money. During the summer, 20 hours of light each day allow as much outdoor activity as any visitor—or resident—can stand.

*A kayaker carefully picks her way past an iceberg near Shoup Glacier.*

It is not unusual for 25 feet of snow to fall on ◀ **A Winter Wonderland** Valdez in one season. The fire hydrants in town sport signs on tall metal rods so firefighters can find them under deep drifts. Valdezans smile at all the snow and keep finding new ways to have fun in it. Winter offers snowmobiling, ice climbing, snowboarding, and skiing—and even an occasional softball game on snowshoes. The annual Ice Climbing Festival in February draws

*Extreme skiing, also called heli-skiing, requires both nerves and skill.*

➤ A record amount of snow—560 inches—fell on Valdez during the winter of 1989–1990. If that much snow fell all at once, it would be as high as a five-storied building.

spectators from far and wide. In March the Winter Carnival features a torchlight cross-country ski parade, dogsled rides, and drive-in movies projected onto a most unusual screen— a 40-foot snowbank. At winter's end, the World Extreme Skiing Championships take place on the slopes of Keystone Canyon and Thompson Pass. Helicopters fly skiers to the mountain peaks, where daredevils plunge down near-vertical cliffs in what looks like suicidal abandon.

Remote, beautiful, and prosperous, Valdez is a place where ageless wilderness and a multi-billion-dollar industry meet. For people and goods coming into Alaska, the Port of Valdez may be the Gateway to the Interior, but for the state's valuable crude oil, Valdez is the gateway to the world.

# GLOSSARY

**balance of trade:** The difference over time between the value of a country's imports and its exports.

**ballast water:** Water held deep within a ship to keep the vessel stable.

**containerization:** A shipping method in which a large amount of goods is packaged in large, standardized containers that are easy to transport.

**fjord:** A narrow sea inlet with steep sides formed by glaciers.

**foreign trade zone (FTZ):** An area near a transportation hub such as a seaport or an airport where goods can be imported without paying import taxes. Foreign traders may store, display, assemble, or process goods in these zones before shipping them to the place where they will eventually be sold. The United States has about 70 foreign trade zones.

**glacier:** A huge mass of ice that flows slowly down a slope or across a plain, scraping out land features as it moves.

**intermodal transportation:** A system of transportation in which goods are moved from one type of vehicle to another, such as from a ship to a train or from a train to a truck, in the course of a single trip.

*Anglers try their luck at one end of the City Dock while a tug muscles a barge into position at the other end of the dock.*

**North American Free Trade Agreement (NAFTA):** A pact between Canada, the United States, and Mexico that went into effect in 1994. The pact created one of the world's largest free-trade zones.

**protectionism:** A trade philosophy of protecting a nation's economy by controlling trade with other countries. Countries that protect their markets often allow only certain types of goods into their country.

**tsunami:** A huge, destructive sea wave caused by underwater earthquakes, landslides, or volcanoes.

## PRONUNCIATION GUIDE

| | |
|---|---|
| *Aleut* | AL-ee-yoot |
| *Alyeska* | al-ee-YEHS-kuh |
| *Beaufort* | BOH-fuhrt |
| *Chugach* | CHOO-gach |
| *Fidalgo, Salvador* | fee-DAHL-goh, sahl-vah-DOHR |
| *Juneau* | JOO-noh |
| *Prudhoe* | PROO-doh |
| *Valdez* | val-DEEZ |

# INDEX

## METRIC CONVERSION CHART

| WHEN YOU KNOW | MULTIPLY BY | TO FIND |
| --- | --- | --- |
| inches | 2.54 | centimeters |
| feet | 0.3048 | meters |
| miles | 1.609 | kilometers |
| square feet | 0.0929 | square meters |
| square miles | 2.59 | square kilometers |
| acres | 0.4047 | hectares |
| pounds | 0.454 | kilograms |
| tons | 0.9072 | metric tons |
| bushels | 0.0352 | cubic meters |
| gallons | 3.7854 | liters |

## ABOUT THE AUTHOR

Nancy Warren Ferrell has written many books and articles for both juvenile and adult markets. In addition to public library work, she has taught elementary school at the Mount Edgecumbe Native Hospital in Sitka, Alaska. A longtime member of the Society of Children's Book Writers and Illustrators, she was one of five judges in the United States in 1992 for the society's Golden Kite Award. In 1995 she received the Contribution to Literacy Award from the Alaska Center for the Book. Ms. Ferrell reviews children's books for a local group in Juneau, Alaska, where she lives with her husband Ed.

## ACKNOWLEDGMENTS

The author owes special gratitude to M. Joseph Leahy, Director of the Valdez Museum, to Curtiss Clifton, Corporate Communications, Alyeska, Valdez, and to Tim Lopez, Valdez Port Director.

Additional thanks go to the following: Kevin Banks, Bruce Webb, and Bill Nebesky of the Northstar Project, Division of Oil and Gas, Anchorage; Brenda Moser, Vice President of Marketing, Petro Star Valdez Refinery, Anchorage; Dave Lee of the Valdez Chamber of Commerce; Mac MacDonald, Valdez Harbormaster; Diana Crisp, Valdez Harbor Office Manager; Ken Morgan, Manager, Solomon Gulch Fish Hatchery; Tamara diFranco, Special Assistant to the Alaska Commissioner of Revenue, Juneau; Walter Flint, Chief of the U.S. Coast Guard in Valdez; Pat Lynn, Editor, *Valdez Star*; Dave Cobb, Mayor of Valdez; Karen McCune of Alyeska Corporate Affairs, Valdez; Jennifer Ruys, Manager, and Tracy Green, International Communication Specialist, Alyeska Media Relations, Anchorage; Mark Moustakis, Operations Advisor, Ship Escort/Response Vessel System; Ryan Sontag, General Manager, North Star Terminal and Stevedore Company, Valdez; Benna Hughey, President, Valdez Native Association; Mark Boudreaux of Exxon Public Affairs, Juneau; Bill Bryson, Principal, Valdez Junior High School; Burt Cottle, Chief of Police, and Janese Chrystal, Administrative Assistant, Valdez Police Department; Lori Cunningham, Trade Specialist, Alaska Division of Trade Development, Anchorage; Jim Hansen, Chief Petroleum Geophysicist, Alaska Oil and Gas, Anchorage; Phil Hubbard, Valdez City Manager; Jim Lethcoe, Valdez Author; Suli Nee of Valdez Employment Service; Bob Romaine, Dean, Prince William Sound Community College, Valdez; Larry Van Bussum of the U.S. Weather Bureau, Juneau; Gregg Williams, Director of Research and Analysis, Department of Labor, Juneau; Pete Carlson, Tourism Development Specialist, Alaska Division of Tourism, Juneau; Laura Walters of Alaska Community and Regional Affairs, Valdez; Colleen Brown of the Alaska Marine Highway, Juneau.